Trade Finance in Progress

Assoc. Prof. Vessela Todorova, PhD
Department of International Economic Relations and Business
Faculty of International Economics and Politics
University of National and World Economy, office 3027
todorova.ves@abv.bg; www.unwe.bg

The publication of this paper is financed through the research project "Export financing and the practice of China Development Bank in Bulgaria" (УНСС № НИД НИ-25/2020) of the University of National and World Economy, Bulgaria

Published by New Generation Publishing in 2023

Copyright © Assoc. Prof. Vessela Todorova, PhD 2023

First Edition

The author asserts the moral right under the Copyright, Designs and Patents Act 1988 to be identified as the author of this work.

All Rights reserved. No part of this publication may be reproduced, stored in a retrieval system or transmitted, in any form or by any means without the prior consent of the author, nor be otherwise circulated in any form of binding or cover other than that which it is published and without a similar condition being imposed on the subsequent purchaser.

ISBN   978-1-80369-708-6

www.newgeneration-publishing.com

New Generation Publishing

Abstract

Trade finance will remain an important component of international financial flows. Historically trade finance has tended to be highly vulnerable in times of crises. Despite the central role played by trade finance, there has been limited analysis of its role in international capital flows, especially during periods of crisis. All institutions and individuals having worked on trade finance have noted the absence of a globally consistent set of statistics. Despite continuous progress regarding guidance, definition and compilation under all institutions most recent statistical manuals, compilation at both national and international levels has been lagging. Twelve years after the Great financial crisis of 2008-2009, the need and the issue of trade finance re-emerged as a matter of urgency.

The global financial crisis in 2008-2009 and particularly the disproportionate drop in trade push the interest of the economists to the issues of trade finance. The importance of trade finance, as an object of the survey, for international transactions is underlined in the working papers. The lack of trade finance is defined as one of the reasons for the decline in trade. The market of trade finance proved to be vulnerable to financial shocks. The lower access to secure, proper and cost-effective trade financing can stop the potential for trade to function as a vector of economic growth.

The COVID-19 crisis is additionally sharpening the barriers in trade finance and in a number of strategic and important directions from the economic development. The uncertainties as a result from the pandemic provoke greater demand for trade finance products. It is supposed that the effects will be stronger than the consequences following the global financial crisis due to the extensive and deep economic effects of COVID-19.

From long-term perspective on international trade finance similar instruments stayed in use more than eight centuries. The bill of exchange has proven to be extremely flexible. Its transformation over time reflected the evolution of global trade finance market. Nowadays the structure of trade finance market is the same as it was the case at its origin. Local banks and local branches of global banks offer a range of products to firms. In combination with credit insurance or guarantees as additional government's support medium-term trade finance (or export finance) has been comparatively more flexible in comparison with short-term trade finance. Trade finance kept its low-risk profile in the turbulence times.

Key Terms: Trade Finance, Documentary Credit, Documentary Collection, Cash-in-advance, Open Account

JEL: F1, F3, F4, G2

Introduction

The economic estimations show that the global financial crisis in 2008-2009 became a reason for USD1trilion shortfall in trade finance in G20 agreeing on a package of USD250 billion in the form of guarantees and insurance to back the trade flows at the 2009 London Summit. Being at the low-risk, high collateral end of the credit spectrum trade finance plays a significant role in 80% of world trade. The importance of trade finance, as an object of the survey, for international transactions is underlined in the working papers. The market of trade finance proved to be vulnerable to financial shocks. As the main idea of the survey, the lower access to secure, proper and cost-effective trade financing can stop the potential for trade to function as a vector of economic growth – unequally interrupting the growth potential of smaller enterprises and developing economies.

Regardless of all hard measures the provisions of trade credit did not restore until 2012. At the same time micro-, small- and medium-sized enterprises (MSMEs) experienced difficulties securing access to trade credit the last 10 years. Global banks refused financing of around 50% of MSME (ICC, 2018). The estimations of Asian Development Bank (ADB, 2019) read that the global shortfall in trade finance is around USD1.5trillion in 2019 – the gap is mainly concentrated in developing and least-developed economies.

The challenges in front of the real economies provoked by Covid-19 might be much harder, analyzers write, in comparison with Global Financial Crisis (Carstens, 2020). ICC forecast estimations (ICC, 2020) show that USD1.9-5.0 trillion capacity in the trade credit market will be necessary for overcoming the potential reduction in global merchandise trade of 13-32% in 2020 (WTO, 2020) and allowing to bring back the global economy. But the required capacity in the bank-intermediated market alone, comprising products such as letters of credit and guarantees, is USD 0.8-1.9 trillion if merchandise trade volumes are to restore in 2021 to levels near to 2019.

Consequently the COVID-19 crisis is additionally sharpening the barriers in trade finance in a number of strategic and important directions from the economic development. The economists argue that the uncertainties as a result from the pandemic provoke greater demand for trade finance products. It is supposed that the effects will be stronger than the consequences following the global financial crisis due to the extensive and deep economic effects of COVID-19. The market of trade finance once again proved to be vulnerable to financial shocks.

1. Literature review

Until the global financial crisis in 2008-2009, only few economic researchers took an interest in international trade finance. On the other hand, there were models on international trade without investigating financial problems. They were considering perfect capital markets, admitting that the cost of external finance is the same as internal finance (Melitz, 2003). In contrast, there was a quite large amount of economic literature on inter-firm trade credit, as suppliers' credits and cash-in-advance without touching its international aspects (Fisman and Love, 2003).

Love et al.(2007) study the question whether trade finance collapses in times of crisis. They study the use and extension of trade credits by firms in Indonesia, South Korea, Malaysia, the Philippines and Thailand during the Asian financial crisis and Mexican firms during the 1994 Peso devaluation. Trade credits, in their research, have double usage - for domestic, as well as for international transactions. The authors do not consider internationally active firms. They show that firms cut out from bank financing in times of liquidity problems cannot find a substitute in the form of trade credit extended by other firms. The explanation is found in the scarcity of financing which has effects over all sources of financing in times of crisis (be it bank credit or inter-firm credit). According to the redistribution theory of Meltzer (1960) and Nilsen (2002) firms redistribute liquidity in the form of trade credit throughout the supply chain; the general lessening of trade credit would affect the whole chain.

Quite soon economic researchers have started to think about financial frictions in the models of international trade. International trade constrains are greater than domestic trade for two reasons. *First*, international transactions are exposed to higher level and a lot of risks, such as the exchange rate risk, the political and non-payment risks. *Second*, the financing needs of internationally active firms are larger, as a result of the time lag between actual production of the good and its delivery.

For the first time financial constraints are included into models of international trade by Manova (2010) and Chaney (2005). They confirm that due to the imperfect contract enforcement and higher non-payment risk, there is a higher mark-up on external finance. As a result, higher cost of external finance may stop firms originally fit to export. That is the case in countries with a low level of financial sector development and for sectors with a high financial vulnerability. Berman and Hericourt (2010) find out that access to finance increases the probability of becoming an exporter by using firm-level survey data from the World Bank for nine emerging and developing countries. Country's financial development is another determinant of firms' probability to become exporters.

The literature on finance and international trade is more extensive in comparison with the literature on financing terms used in international trade, which is new, but expanding. Schmidt-Eisenlohr (2013) created a model describing the compromises faced by trading partners while choosing financing terms. When the cost of financing and the quality of contract enforcement in the exporter's country are higher than the same in the importer's country, open account terms are more preferable than cash-in-advance financing terms. In the case of low quality contract enforcement in both countries and low letter of credit fees, the letter of credit is the most preferred financing term.

The Schmidt-Eisenlohr model (2013) is extended by Antras and Foley (2015) by a dynamic setting showing how the choice of financing terms in international trade also depends on the duration of the relationship between the trading partners. As repeated interaction helps develop trust the use of cash-in-advance financing decreases with the duration of the relationship. The authors tested their model prediction by using data from a large US poultry firm.

Demir and Javorcik (2018) investigate another factor that matters for the choice of financing term in international trade. To show that an increase in the level of market competition leads exporters to extend more trade credit to their buyers the authors investigate firm-level customs data disaggregated by financing terms. As a result, there is an increase in open account terms financing.

The usage of letter of credits across countries is explored by Niepmann and Schmidt-Eisenlohr (2017). The authors use SWIFT data, covering nearly 90% of global letter-of-credit transactions, presenting an extensive set of empirical calculations over various country-level characteristics that affect the use of letter-of-credit. Unlike them, the essence of Crozet et al (2020) is product-level factors that affect the intensity of the usage of letter-of-credit in international trade. As a result from their analysis products that rely more on trade insurance registered a greater decline in exports to destinations affected by the Great Recession than other products did. The supply of letter-of-credits is negatively influenced.

The choice of financing terms by trading partners is also influenced by the banking sector development. By detailed information about imports transactions from Columbia Ahn and Sermiento (2019) prove that import was significantly influenced by bank liquidity shocks via the letter of credit channel during the Great Recession. Other authors, Demir et al. show that firms use letter-of-credits less (more) intensively when exporting to countries for which the cost of letter-of-credits increased (decreased) after the Basel II adoption by the usage of mandatory adoption of the Basel II framework in Turkey, affecting the cost of holding letter-of-credits by banks.

After proving the importance of access to finance for international trade transactions, the next question is whether specific trade finance instruments can help to overcome financial constraints. Letters of credit, supplier credit, and cash-in-advance are used in international trade strongly. Eck et al. (2012) find out that 96% of all exporters among the German firms use supplier credit through firm-level survey data. Moreover, exporters and importers also use a higher share of supplier credit on their inputs and receive a higher share of sales as advance payments than domestic traders. Then the next question comes - why internationally active firm use trade credits so actively?

Inter-firm trade finance gives a quality signal which lower the uncertainty of trading internationally prove Eck et al. (2012). By the inherent quality of getting better the information on trading partners, trade credits are facilitating access of the firms involved to credit in general. On the other hand, Engemann et al. (2012) find that supplier credits may lead to more bank credits for financially constrained and internationally active firms. For that reason trade credits may be interpreted as complements not only substitutes to traditional bank credits. Furthermore, the positive relationship between export credit insurance and trade is investigated by Van der Veer (2010) and Felbermayer and Yalcin (2011). Export credit insurance data before that is analyzed by Egger and Url (2006), Moser et al.(2008).

The international trade in goods and services is impossible without the day-to-day lifeblood of trade finance. More precisely, trade finance provides fluidity and security needed for the movement process of goods and services (Auboin and Meier-Ewert, 2008).

2. Trade Finance and Financial Crisis.

The drop in global trade during the financial crisis 2008-2009 outpaced the drop in GDP due to a factor that was much larger than anticipated under standard models. Economists have found potential reasons in trade restrictions, a lack of trade finance, vertical specialization, and the composition of trade.

To determine the role of credit in the Japanese financial crises Amiti and Weinstein (2011) examine firm-level data from 1990 through 2010. They proved a causal link between the two by their data, which matches firm's exports to the health of their banks. They find that the foreign sales of firms, working with banks which suffered greatly, drop more than their domestic sales. They estimated that the trade finance channel accounts for about 20% of the decline in Japanese exports in the financial crises in 2008-2009. Both authors give an explanation of why exporters, more than any other producers, are more reliant on credit in general, and trade credit and guarantees in particular. For the reason that a small part of world trade is paid cash or in advance, exporters rely on their banks and insurance companies to advance working capital to produce the goods for export and /or assume the payment, counterparty, transport, political, exchange rate and all other risks, characterized trade transactions. Moreover, multinational enterprises and firms that export mostly by air are less affected by an impairment of their main bank's health. A large part of multinational trade, which exhibit less risk, is intra-firm. The relation of the time needed for shipment and the firm's working capital needs is the explanation for that thesis. In other words, the shorter the lag between production and payment, the less finance is a problem.

Chor and Manova (2012) also investigate how credit conditions work as a channel through which the crisis led to the collapse in trade by using data on US imports. Measured by their interbank interest rates, the export to the US of countries with tighter credit markets is falling during the recent financial crisis. The effect is rising for financially vulnerable industries. Chor and Manova (2012) categorized financially vulnerable industries as those that look for extensive financing, have limited access to trade credit, or have few collateralizable assets. The result of their research is that financially vulnerable industries became especially sensitive to the costs of credit during the peak of the financial crisis.

The result of Bricongne et. al. (2012) is the quite the same. The group of economists argues that highly dependent sectors on external finance have been hit by the financial crisis with the largest drop in their export activity.

In their paper the authors are testing whether firms with heterogeneous characteristics have been affected differently through the crisis by using monthly data for individual French exporters at the product and destination level. Small and less productive firms may be more adversely hit by the crisis than larger and more productive firms. Bricongne et. al. (2012) discovers that small and large firms have been similarly hit by the crisis. Consequently, programs to increase the availability of trade finance do not have to be directed to certain groups of firms but rather to specific industries.

Iacovone and Zavacka (2009) are other authors, who are investigating these problems – more precisely the impact of bank credit on exports during crisis times and how various export sectors differ in their need for external financing. Their result shows that the most exposed sectors should be hit harder during a banking crisis or in other words – during a crisis the export of sectors more dependent on external finance grow significantly less than other sectors. By using data from 23 banking crisis episodes involving both developed and developing countries during the period 1980-2000, the authors separate the impact of banking crisis on export growth from that of other exogenous shocks (i.e. demand shocks). The result confirms only for sectors depending more heavily on bank finance as opposed to inter-firm finance. The effect of banking crisis on exports is strong and a compliment to external demand shocks. The effect of "demand-side" shocks is independent and it is very important for sectors producing durable goods.

The thesis of all of these papers is contradicting to the thesis of Love et al. (2007) that trade credit cannot serve as a substitute to bank credit in times of crisis. The reason for that contradiction is the different focus - Iacovone and Zavacka (2009) are focusing on exporters whereas Love et al. (2007) do not explicitly look at international transactions. In other words, in the local banking crises analyzed by Love et al. (2007) exporters have the possibility to get financing through trade credits from their international trading partners unaffected from the crisis. Although in times of global financial crisis, as it was the crisis in 2008-2009, firms financing by trade credits also have been affected by the crisis as shown by Chor and Manova (2012).

Ahn (2011) develops a model to show the different nature of international relative to domestic trade finance to investigate theoretically the reason of the effect of a lack of trade finance on trade compared to GDP during the crisis in 2008-2009. In the model banks interact more with domestic firms. From the banks' point of view international transactions are more risky than purely domestic transactions. That is the reason for the usage of letters of credit for international transactions and not for national transactions by firms. By using letter of credit the two banks – the bank of the exporter and the bank of the importer, are screening the exporting firm and the importer located in their countries. Being the transaction international, no bank has to screen a foreign firm. According to the author, part of the disproportionate drop in trade during the financial crisis can be explained by banks first cutting international trade finance and by exclusive use of letters of credit in international trade.

Other investigation works do not prove the thesis of the role of the trade finance in the great collapse of the financial crisis in 2008-2009. Paravisini et al. (2011) is such an example. According to the authors, the increased cost of working capital affects overall production, be it for domestic markets or exports. Using data for the US and Belgium, Levchenko et al. (2011) and Behrens et al. (2011) also show how trade credit did not play a significant role in the large fall in trade relative to GDP in the global financial crisis in 2008-2009.

The global financial crisis in 2008-2009 and particularly the disproportionate drop in trade push the interest of the economists to the issues of trade finance. The importance of trade finance for international transactions is underlined in the working papers. And the lack of trade finance is defined as one of the reasons for the decline in trade.

3. Trade finance and the Covid-19 Crisis.

The wake of Covid-19 Crisis

In a world of global value chains where goods cross borders plenty of times, international trade is disproportionate influenced by any drop in the world economy. The Great Trade Collapse, as a result of the 2008-2009 financial crises, is such an example.

The downturn, caused by the Covid-19 pandemic, is not different. The French exports dropped by 38% in March 2020 relative to historical patterns, the latest available data read (Demir and Javorcik, 2020). The decline in Germany was 23%, while 25% and 12% in Turkey and in the US, respectively. Due to the Eurozone slowdown French and German exports have been declining. Their March drop was larger than the pre-pandemic trend.

There are many factors for the decrease of trade in periods of the economic slowdown. The decline in demand for durables (Levchenko et al, 2010; Eaton et al, 2016) is the one of great importance. The next factors include the increased protectionism (Evenette, 2009) and the interaction between uncertainty and higher ordering costs (relative to domestic) inputs (Berman et al., 2019). The worsened access to credit during financial crises and trade finance are also of great importance (Ahn., 2011; Amiti and Weinstein, 2011; Chor and Manova, 2012; Paravisini et al., 2015).

The increased risk of non-payment or non-delivery of pre-paid goods is another important reason which means that unsecured flows are less resilient than insured flows. On 28 April 2020 the Financial Times reported that "the current crisis brings with it a significant increase in late payments and additional risks that our client may face unpaid invoices as certain buyers may present heightened levels of risk of non-payment and deteriorate credit worthiness and that the financing available for trade flows in emerging and frontier markets has dropped even more than volume of trade." `The increased uncertainty and inability to secure flows by using trade finance instruments, such as letters of credit, worsen the international trade. The opportunities for trade finance are declining in emerging markets in the past decade although the current downtrend is not followed by a financial crisis (WTO and IFC, 2019).

Historically, losses on trade receivables have been relatively small in comparison with those on other asset classes (International Chamber of Commerce, 2018). During recessions, including the global financial crisis, trade credit has often proved to be a resilient source of funding (CGFS,

2014; Coulibaly et al.. 2011). But the pandemic presents a perfect storm for supply chains.

The pandemic has hit real activity directly, rather than working primarily. In the case of the global financial crises, it was through stresses in the banking sector. Central banks do not have enough direct levers to cope with non-financial corporations` financial stress as they have for banks. That makes the supporting measures more difficult (Carstens, 2020). The Covid-19 shock is more synchronized across sectors and countries, with buyers and suppliers being affected at the same time. In such circumstances the inter-firm lending in the form of trade credit to soften the effect of the economic impact is likely to be reduced. During an aggregate shock on the scale of Covid-19 the mechanism of the large firms acting as liquidity insurers against idiosyncratic shocks inside their supply chain in normal times (Boissay and Group, 2013) may not work in the wake of the crisis.

The analyzers suppose the longer and more global supply chains to transform even the largest companies "as weak as the weakest link". For example, the auto industry may have been hit notably hard due to knock-on effects along supply chains (Miller et al., 2020).

Being tested some credit risk mitigation arrangements provoke uncertainty during the Covid-19 crisis. For example "the reverse factoring", which allows large buyers to receive cash from banks for their payables until payments, are called in by their suppliers. The reverse factoring creates potential for the firms to hide borrowing from banks as trade credits in the absence of disclosure requirements. Such cash is earmarked for suppliers and does not provide the liquidity buffer that cash would normally provide although firms can rise their cash holdings (Jafari and Kalousova, 2018; Eaglesham, 2020).

In the wake of the Covid-19 crisis there are other sources of vulnerability already known in the economic literature. After sharp increase of the dollar (USD) exchange rate trade finance and the global value chains deteriorate. The changes of the USD exchange rate are negatively correlated with the global trade finance volumes (Boissay et al., 2020). The financial channel of the exchange rate is the most important factor, influencing this relation. The sensitivity of USD credit supply to the broad dollar exchange rate is the reason for worsening the USD financial condition after rising of the USD exchange rate (Bruno and Shin, 2019; Avdjiev et al., 2019). There is relationship between the increase of the USD exchange rate and the worsen credit conditions.

The stress in the banking system as a result from the sharp increase of the USD provokes effects over trade finance in the early stages of the Covid-19. Mitigating the influence of USD credit changes is an important protection of global value chains from pandemic`s economics collapse given the prevalence of USD in trade finance. The expansions of central bank dollar swap lines are possible measures to mitigate USD liquidity conditions and to keep trade finance.

The challenges in front of the real economies provoked by Covid-19 might be much harder, analyzers write, in comparison with Global Financial Crisis (Carstens, 2020). The support to large firms might be organized by central bank's corporate bond purchase programs (Adelino et al., 2020). But for smaller firms in the supply chain more direct support in the form of grants and loan guarantees are better instrument to soften the effects of the shock. For purchase trade receivables and raising the cash government-guaranteed bank loans could be included as an alternative. Using different central bank facilities these loans could even be securitized and financed.

Private parties are supported by special financial infrastructure provided by the governments. Small suppliers in Mexico have the opportunity to use their receivables from big buyers to receive working capital financing by reverse factoring facility without providing funding or factoring services by NAFIN Development Bank. Authorities in Europe raised the domestic credit insurers' loss absorption capacity by direct involvement of private funds. About 14% of trade receivables of credit insurers are exposed to risk and influenced by the pandemic (Boissay et al., 2020).

The higher exposure of banks and other intermediaries to trade finance and the greater part of USD denominated trade financing define the international dimension of the Covid-19 effects. The governments have already taken measures to increase the capacity of export credit agencies by expanding working capital programs and new facilities to support exporters and importers, especially SMEs (OECD, 2020).

The Covid-19 Crisis changed image

The Coronavirus pandemic has had a devastating effect on economies and societies worldwide. The estimations of OECD read a reduction of global GDP by 3.4% (OECD, Mar 2021) and a contraction of global trade by 10.9% (OECD, Dec 2020). The governments were pressed to mobilize and develop policies to counter the economic impact of the pandemic. Proved successful in countering the decrease in private market trade finance the governments looked for programs to relieve the trade disruptions created by Covid-19.

Unlike most recessions the Covid-19 crisis represents a single unforeseeable shock. (John Hassier, Jul 2020) This means that governments could not be able to solely rely on the experience knowledge from past crises to overcome its negative effects. The type and size of all disturbances to the trade world and especially to the trade financing world differs from those in the past. For that reason the governments must start with their identification before mobilizing different tools at disposal, as export support programs.

As comprehensive data on trade finance does not exist, information remains limited on the level and the type of the disruptions that has emerged.

OECD surveys indicators suggest that ST trade finance is facing access problems, as increased costs of ST financing for SMEs and higher rates of rejected applications. They predict resilience of MLT financing. The number of MLT export credit transactions decreases by 34% in volume and 15% in number in 2020. The indicators show a drop in large projects but not in standard MLT business. Should the pandemic continue and weigh further on cash flows of MLT projects the resilience may not last.

4. Definition of Trade Finance.

Payment for the exchange of goods and services is made in several ways. In the simplest forms the seller is paid by cash in advance or payment is made at delivery. Some forms of financing, as the deferred payment, enable the buyer to pay the seller over time. Such financing of trade takes many different forms and may involve financial institutions.

Trade finance products typically include intra-firm financing, inter-firm financing, and some special tools are – advance payment guarantees/bonds, cash-in-advance, documentary collection (DC), letters of credit (LC), open account, performance bonds, and export credits insurance or guarantees.

Figure 1: Payment-Risk Diagram

PAYMENT RISK DIAGRAM

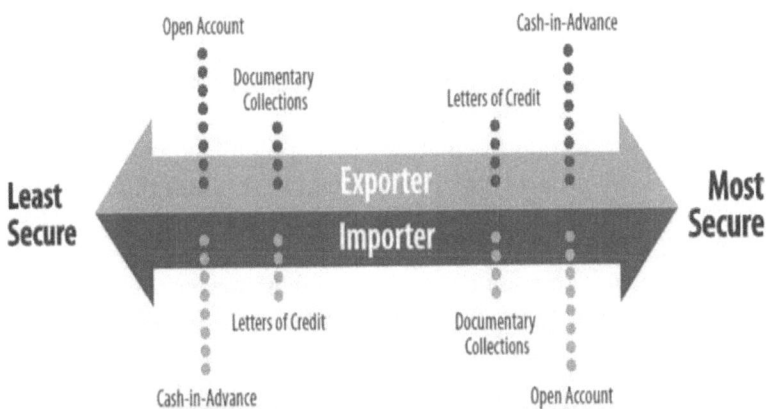

Source: US International Trade Administration
(https://www.trade.gov/methods-payment)

Trade finance consists of various instruments. In Figure 1 the arrangement of the main trade finance instruments is according their payment-risk profile between the seller (exporter) and buyer (importer) in an international trade transaction. Thus, in order for policies on trade finance to be effective, one has to know when which form of trade finance is used in international trade. Complete data on how different types of transactions are financed is not easy to find. For that reason empirical studies have rely on whatever data exists, aggregate sectoral, country-level or firm-level data.

The optimal choice between different payment conditions in recent papers is connecting with cross-country difference in contract enforcement, cost and availability of trade finance. The best option for cash –in-advance is the situation when a good is exported to a country with weak contract enforcement (Antras & Foley, 2011, and Shmidt-Eisenlohr, 2012). The use of letters of credit decreases any incentive to default (moral hazard) when the transaction is between two countries with weak contract enforcement. Such incentive may appear when the importer receives the good payment. On the other hand the moral hazard may be reduced through guarantees by the bank of the importer on its ability to pay. The idea is that enforcement between banks is easier than between two trading partners (Olsen, 2010). Moreover trading partners want to minimize financing cost. Hence the financing mode depends on which firm has lower financing costs, i.e. better bank credit opportunities. (Ahn, 2011)

There are empirically studies of these theories. Smchmidt-Eisenlohr (2012) finds that two countries trade less with each other if the cost for financing is higher by using panel data on bilateral trade flows. The effect gets higher with the distance to the destination country and increases the time between production and payment to some extent because of transportation take times. In such situation the need of credit is higher and more expensive.

Glady and Potin (2011) confirm that firms prefer letters of credit in their trade transactions with countries with a high risk of default with respect to the choice between financing instruments. As a result from the SWIFT data analyses, when exporting to countries with s high commercial default risk than countries with a low commercial default risk letters of credit appear to be used four times more intensively. Moreover, letters of credit would be used more often when the parties in the transaction are located in countries with higher financial market development where fees probably are lower.

The reaction of institutions on choice between different financial modes is analyzed by Antras and Foley (2011) using transaction data from U.S. based exporter of frozen poultry, which includes financing terms by transaction. First, supplier credits and cash-in-advance are the most commonly used financing terms by this company. Only one fifth of the value of the transactions involves bank-intermediated financing. Second, the institutional environment of the destination country is of great importance for the choice of the financing terms. Cash-in-advance is the best choice for prime exports to countries with weak contract enforcement. But cash-in-advance is less likely to be used when trading partners establish a narrow relationship.

In brief the economic researches conclude that the institutional context and financial sector development are the two important factors determined the choice of trade financing instruments.

The level of risk of trade across international borders is higher than that of trading within national borders. Shipping goods internationally needs dealing with trading partners who are located in different countries, speak a different language, and are subject to different laws and regulations. International trade involves longer transit times that expose trading partners to risks ranging from exchange rate movement and demand uncertainty to political instability.

By choosing one of the four financial terms (figure 1) – cash in advance, open account, letter of credit and documentary collection, trading partners need to decide how to allocate those risks. Under *cash-in-advance terms*, the exporter receives a payment before the ownership of goods is transferred to the importer or even before the goods are shipped. The importer faces the risk of never receiving the pre-paid goods. Under *open account terms*, goods are shipped and delivered before a payment is made by the importer. So it is the exporter, who bears the risk of never receiving a payment. The letter of credit terms allow both parties to transfer the risk on to a bank in exchange for a fee. Under *a letter of credit*, the bank of the importer commits to make the payment to the exporter upon the verification of the fulfillment of the terms and conditions stated in the letter of credit. So the exporter is sure that payment will be received. Before the goods arrival, the importer does need to make payment.

Documentary collection is the other financing term including bank intermediation. Under documentary collection the exporter trust the collection of payment to its bank. Together with payment instructions the bank of the exporter sends the documents to the importer`s bank. Since the banks do not provide a payment guarantee, documentary collection is much cheaper than the letter of credit. By the proper instruction the banks are contributing to some extent to risk mitigation.

The risk of non-payment and non-delivery of prepaid goods is rising in an unexpected adverse economic shock, such as the Covid-19 pandemic. The export transactions backed by letter of credit and documentary collection is expected to be more resilient than all other financing terms. The export backed by letter of credit and documentary collection terms is supposed to be relatively stable (Demir and Javorcik, 2020).

Among these products, a traditional distinction is made between short-term (ST) trade finance products and medium- and long-term (MLT) export financing/guarantees. The ST trade finance provides for differed payment over a period of less than one year (usually less 180 days), while MLT period can be extended with repayment terms reaching, or even exceeding, ten years. The ST financing facilities are specifically used for trade in commodities, intermediate or consumer goods. Contrary to them, MLT financing techniques are preferred in the case of capital goods or goods with a longer useful life. They are very often part of projects with their own revenues that can be used to service the debt as a result of importer project finance. ST trade finance is supplied mainly by private banks (banokintermediated trade financing) and by firms (firm-to-firm or intra-firm credit) (Chauffour and Farole, 2009).

Although the reliable and detailed information on international trade finance is difficult to find, studies estimate that bank-intermediated trade finance accounts for 10% to 30% of world trade, with the remainder being organized by inter-firm trade credits through open account trading (Lotte van Wersch, 2019). The active participants in this market are commercial lenders such as multinational banks, local commercial banks, non-bank lenders, credit insurers and official export credit agencies (ECAs) backed by their governments.

4.1 Trade Credit and Trade Finance

A great part of the working capital of most firms is defined as an "accounts receivable". That is the money owed by customers in the supply chain. Accounts receivable are matched partly by "accounts payable" on the liabilities side of the balance sheet. Or they are the money owed to suppliers further up in the chain. The interconnected chain of receivables and payables is compared with the glue that binds supply chains together in the real economy and maintains their operation, both domestically and internationally (Carstens, 2020; Kim and Shin, 2012).

Aiming to provide credit to customer firms, the receivables may be financed by non-financial corporation with their own resources. All these relations are defined as "trade credit". As an alternative they may choose "factoring" to relieve banks' exposure and that to other financial institutions. As a short term financing via factoring, receiving immediate cash firms sell their accounts receivable at a discount to a third party known as the "factor", which is typically a bank. External financing is mainly common for importers and exporters. And the term "trade finance" is used collectively for all such arrangements facilitating international trade.

In the world of interconnected payables and receivables, firms borrow from their suppliers and lend to their customers. Trade credit chains are created. They are functioning in parallel to the flow of goods along supply chains. For non-financial corporations trade credit is a significant form of funding. The volume of trade payables can be compared with that of outstanding corporate bonds. It is about one third of non-financial corporation's outstanding bank loans (Boissay et al., 2020). They are mainly oriented to financing of inputs. Therefore they are not so influenced by the cyclical ups and downs of corporate loans and bonds. As a result, their volume is stable and about 20% of GDP over the past 25 years.

In comparison with trade payables, trade finance, measured by the share of cross-border factoring in total factoring, has constantly rising up over the past two decades (Boissay et al., 2020). The increasing of international trade, mainly the lengthening of global value chains, is in parallel with the rising long-term trend of trade finance. Trade finance has become more significant in the context of global value chains since financing needs increase with the length of supply chains (Bruno et al, 2018; Bruno and Shin, 2019).

4.2 Mechanism of Trade Finance.

Trade finance mechanism is supporting two basic aspects of the trading process – risk mitigation and liquidity.

Any economic exchange is characterized by the element of risk. Principally to what extent the seller will succeed to deliver and the buyer to pay or accept, the goods or services as agreed in the trade contract. All these risks are rising in an international trading environment provoked by factors as macroeconomic volatility, political risk, information asymmetry and moral hazard. As a result the traders are using different facilities to mitigate and/or compensate for these risks.

Usually exporters face a gap between the time of the done production costs and the time of payment of the importer. A liquidity gap appears, getting greater by the payment terms granted to buyers as a period of days or weeks in which to realize the payment. This time period is getting longer in international trade due to the necessary time for products transportation to their markets. Firms are looking for credits to overcome the liquidity gap.

The great number of trade finance instruments involves credits extended bilaterally between firms in a supply chain or between different units of separate firms. Banks also play a central role in facilitating trade. They provide finance provisions, different facilities, organize and manage the payment mechanisms such as telegraphic transfers and documentary letters of credit (L/Cs). Different entities take part in the activities of the banks, such as export credit agencies, private insurers, and multilateral development banks.

Export credit agencies (ECAs). They are quasi-governmental agencies that in general provide cover in the form of partial or comprehensive insurance and guarantees against counterparty risk. In practice ECAs do not provide direct funding to traders. By guarantying the trade financing to the exporters they are enlarging the role of the banks.

Private Insurers. The role of the private insurers in the market as providers of trade credit risk, political risk insurance and bonding facilities is rising recently. Especially in providing short-term credit insurance they are standing higher in comparison with ECAs in all OECD countries, with exception of Japan and Canada. (Chauffour and Faraole, 2009). Insurance policies are normally used by exporters as collateral to enlarge the working capital or to unlock accounts receivables. Banks also often hold insurance policies on their L/C business lines.

Multilateral development banks (MDBs). The World Bank, International Financial Corporation (IFC) and a lot of regional development banks (i.e., EBRD, Inter-American DB and African DB) deal with formal trade facilitation programs to support their member countries. These programs extend the role of developing country banks. By issuing guarantees they are providing risk mitigation of the delivered trade financing in restricted credit lines conditions. The customers of these programs are mainly classified as small- and medium-size enterprises with no minimum transaction size.

Table 1: Overview of Trade Finance Products

Category	Products
Inter-firm/Supply Chain Financing	• Open Account
"Traditional" Bank Financing	• Investment Capital • Working Capital • Pre-export Finance
Payment Mechanism and Liquidity	• Letter of Credit Issuance • Supplier Credit • Buyer Credit • Countertrade • Factoring and Forfaiting
Risk Management	• Advance Payment Guarantees • Performance Bond • Refund Guarantees • Hedging
Export Credit Insurance/ Guarantees	• Export Credit Insurance • Export Credit Guarantees

Table 1 presents the main products included in discussion of trade finance – from inter-firm credit to traditional forms of bank-provided credit (for liquidity and investment) and products for mitigating the risk and the liquidity gap in international trade. L/Cs is the most often used international trade finance products. In the L/Cs process the importers and exporters entrust the whole process and the mitigation of the counterparty risk to their respective banks.

There are a lot of differences between trade finance and the rest forms of credit (e.g. investment and working capital) with important economic effects during periods of financial crisis. The most important one is that trade finance may be received not only through third party financial institutions but also through inter-firm transactions. According to traditional economic theory if the company has no access to bank credit, due to high implicit inter-firm trade credit costs, it can obtain financing through suppliers. (Petersen & Raghuram, 1997)

The prevalent usage of inter-firm trade finance is a result of its certain features. It is allowing trade partners to better mitigating risk than third parties. *Informational advantage* is the first specific feature. Trade partners are in better position than banks in assessing the risk of non-performance, non-payment, or strategic default. Informational advantage hypotheses in a restricted way may explain the extension of credit depending on the nature of products and services traded and on the market power of suppliers and buyers. (Giannetti, Burkart & Ellingsen, 2007; Fabbri & Klapper, 2009) The second advantage is *the trust*, or more specifically *encapsulated interest*. Having greater interest the buyer stay in business and continue to work with them, suppliers may be more willing than banks to extend credit. (Giannetti, Burkart & Ellingsen, 2007)

Not being in business of financing, the aim of trading firms offering credit is to raise the competitiveness of their basic product or service. They extend credit on terms that allow it to maximize the profits of their core offering. As a result, the market power is depending on the dilemma of extending or receiving interfirm trade credit. The size of the competitiveness in the market and the industry structure of the suppliers determine their actions. Not so powerful suppliers are extending less credit and similarly powerful suppliers are demanding more favorable terms. The economic literature argue that firms with less market power extend more credit (Fabbri & Klapper, 2009), and that a customer that generate a large share of its supplier's profits tends to have more credit extended to them (Giannetti, Burkart & Ellingsen, 2007). Giannetti, Burkart & Ellingsen (2007) also find that suppliers of services tend to be highly differentiated, extend more credit than suppliers of standardized goods. Being practically impossible to divert services present no "moral hazard" and limit the risk of strategic default. Thus, emerging market exporters, being relatively small and selling mainly standardized products, are possible to be forced to extend favorable credit terms and have not got possibilities to demand similar terms of their input suppliers.

Trade finance – whether offered through banks or within the supply chain, is comparatively illiquid in comparison with a standard credit line or working capital loan. It cannot easily be diverted for another usage. The high collateralization is the other difficulty – credit and insurance are provided directly against the sale of specific products or services, whose value is calculated and secured.[1] It means that the risk of strategic default on trade finance is low. In suppler-extended credit the risk of trade finance is even lower. Buyers are less likely to default on supplier-extended credit, because of the liquidity problem. The bank credit is somewhat more liquid. "The moral hazard" is greater in the case of bank financing. In the event of non-payment, the supplier is obtaining higher value from liquidizing the collateralized asset (i.e. goods being traded) than the bank. The nature of the product being traded is important in both cases – the differentiated the product the less it poses a moral hazard to buyers (Giannetti, Burkart & Ellingsen, 2007) and the greater the relative liquidation advantage that would accrue to supplier over bank (Fabbri &Menichini, 2009).

Another specific feature of trade finance, connected with greater potential risk, is its international context. Cross border trades face *macro-level risks* which can influence the value of return (e.g., exchange rate fluctuations, changes in policy) and the possibilities of default (e.g., conflicts, political upheaval). In parallel they face specific *counterparty risks* in relation with greater difficulty of enforcement across borders, intensified in many developing countries by poorly functioning institutions, especially legal systems (Menichini, 2009). Weak cross-border enforcement increases the risk of strategic default on the part of suppliers, creating the problem of "credible commitment" across borders (Ellingsen & Vlachos, 2009). Finally, the cross-border nature of trade finance limits the assessment of the counterparty credit risk. These risks may be mixed in the case of supplier-extended credit, by the fact that greater part of suppliers operate in "credit chains" – i.e. firms which extend credit to their suppliers in turn have credit extended to them from their suppliers. Working capital provided by inter-firm credits to support production and trade is critical. At the same time they are vulnerable to shocks as they can quickly create problems across the chain (Kiyotaki & Moore, 1997; Raddatz, 2008), strengthening the systemic risk.

---

[1] That is not true in all cases. Such products are perishable (i.e. their value erodes quickly) and extremely differentiated (there is little or no market value outside the intended buyer). The services are not generally able to be collateralized.

5. Trade Finance in Progress.

As the oldest field of international finance, trade finance comprises all instruments and methods necessary for obtaining large amounts of capital for short time financing international activities and covering the risks of all participants (merchants and firms) in the international trade. From the very beginning of the international trade history, exporters and importers have tried to find new techniques for lowering the risks specific for long-distance international transactions in the organization of great amount of working capital. They are produced either by banks, known as "bank-intermediated trade finance" in the modern literature, or by exporting and importing firms, called "inter-firm" trade credit.

From middle Ages up to the present day the structure and governance of this market have been reshaping in parallel with the evolution of international monetary and financial system. Trade credit instruments and the role played by banks in the main international financial centers in financing international trade have also been evolving over time.

From historical point of view, the bill of exchange was the most universal instrument broadcasted in the middle Ages. At first, issued by merchant and banking firms, consisted of specific assets, bills of exchange have been used as instruments of private credit for the financing of international trade.

> As a private written order by one party to another to pay a given sum of money at a given date, the *bills of exchange* are also credit instruments, not only means of national or international payment, as it is the cheque.

The standardization of the trade finance products rose up from the sixteenth century onwards and progressively the process of centralization of the international trade financing around the main trading centers of Antwerp, Amsterdam and London was on. In the nineteenth century London was transformed into global center for international trade finance, a large part of which was financed through the London money market.

The disintegrated structure of the global trade finance market evaluated during the interwar and post-war years. The decentralized market in the form of trade finance products issued by banks in the exporters' and importers' countries recovered in the post-1970 period.

5.1 Trade Finance after 1000 AD in the period of 1100-1800.

The information for the emergence of trade finance is not so much in the Antiquity however it was present in the early civilizations of the Middle East being one of the pillars of the early banking systems of the Greek Mediterranean.

The available information could be determined on the re-emergence of trade finance in the West after 1000 AD. Until the 13th century, international trade was basically financed by specific native lending activities. The trade organization was still represented as "caravan trade", in which the financing was organized through the creation of special partnerships among fellow citizens. The organization and financing itself happened on a bilateral foot although the links between the entrepreneurs' place of origin with an international trading center.

- *Features of Medieval bill of exchange.*

During the 13th century, when the merchants started to establish permanent networks of correspondents, the trade started to change its structure in the form of "sedentary trade". Such phenomenon was typical for Italian companies (except the Germans, Baltic regions, extra-European places, without Constantinople) (De Roover, Raymond, 1953). Within the new trading model, the trade flows were organized multilaterally among the different vertexes of each single correspondent network. The organization of trade continued to be among groups of fellow citizens on a greater scale than before and the funding derived from such "clans". That was the way of emergence of the future main instrument of international trade finance – the bill of exchange.

The original bill of exchange was a certificate, not a standardized credit instrument, of a private credit contract between two local agents, to be presented to a foreign correspondent.

Being not standardized instrument, it was not possible to trade with medieval bills of exchange on an open market. In the medieval period the nature of financing trade is quite specific. A good example is the medieval bill of exchange, known as "exchange on Venice" (cambium ad Venetias). In the 15th century the international trade to and from Venice was financed by Florentine capital in the form of non-marketable local credit contracts, issued by Florentine companies. Companies like the Medici bank started to offer to Florentine investors a new financial product, denominated in Florentine currency with return indexed on Venetian interest rate. (De Roover, Raymond, 1974)

> *Venice* became the first stable commercial center, a crossroad between Western Europe and the Eastern Mediterranean (Mueller, Reinhold C.,1997), in which Florentine trade and banking companies created branches, playing important role in the financing trade flows.

- *The Appearance of Negotiable Trade Finance Instruments.*

In the early modern era the importing and exporting firms started to lend directly to each other by purchasing their bills after the introduction of negotiability. The nature of the bill of exchange changed. The bill transformed from a certificate of a local credit contract into an exchange-traded financial instrument. In the mid-18th century the financing of trade transactions was organized through credits lent between firms themselves specialized in overseas trade.

In the first half of the 16th century – from the 1510s until the 1560s, Antwerp played the role of commercial metropolis of Western Europe. The management of inter-group liquidity for financing the trade was the advantage of network companies in comparison with the more primitive traders. They had to mobilize quickly the returns of their sales and to convert them into commodity for re-export. To that aim, Northern traders insisted on getting the recognition of the principle of negotiability of credit instruments by the Antwerp authorities, which transferred to the bearer the juridical protection previously granted exclusively to the original creditor. The necessary condition for trade finance to overcome local dimensions was the negotiability.

> The principle had been permitted by decrees of Charles V's in the Low Countries[2] in 1537. Next decades bills of exchange were influenced by the practice of endorsement.(De Roover, Raymond,1953)

The new international standard – the "Antwerp custom", was established as a result of the role of Antwerp as new European trade center by the early 17th century. The negotiable bill of exchange had transformed into basic instrument for financing the intra-European trade. Finally the location of the borrower and the lender had been separated.

In the meantime, the emergence of Amsterdam as leading trade center pushes the transforming the bill on Amsterdam into an increasingly popular instrument. (Gillard, Lucien, 2004) During the 17th and 18th centuries the

---

[2] *The Low Countries* comprise the coastal Rhine–Meuse–Scheldt delta region in Western Europe, whose definition usually includes the modern countries of Luxembourg, Belgium and the Netherlands.

organization of trade finance in terms of geographic and demographic aspect became with free-entry in comparison with late medieval age, in which the list of banks, determined by oligopolistic Italian companies, was very limited.

The introduction of negotiability shifted the architecture of the trade finance market with substantial evolution of trade finance instruments in parallel but their circulation remains restricted. The payment of reciprocal debt among merchant firms was organized by the appearance of new negotiable bill of exchange. Nevertheless international trade was mainly financed on a decentralized basis. Specialized agents had extended credits in the exporters` and importer`s countries.

5.2 The Trade finance in the period of 1800-1900. The Bill on London.

Deep transformation of the global trade finance market happened after the appearance and gradual internationalization of the large discount market for bills of exchange in London from the second of the 18th century to the early 20th century. Being highly liquid and secure money market instruments bills of exchange drawn on London City began to circulate across the globe and to finance trade transactions around the whole world. A great number of participants from the country and all over the world took part in the trade with such highly-standardized products, issued by specialized agents, around one financial center. They were a brand-new instrument, the so-called *inland bill*, issued at first by the London discount market. Britain played a central role in financing the global trade boom of the second half of the 19th century and in regulating firm`s access to trade finance.

Drawn and payable in England the inland bill was only domestic credit instrument. The inland bill became a very popular means of payment for domestic transactions in England. It was exchanged on the constantly increasing discount market, which was soon used for financing international trade as well.

> London offset Amsterdam both as intra-continental and inter-continental trade center in the end of Napoleonic Wars.[3] At that time intra-continental trade finance differed from inter-continental trade. Negotiable bill of exchange was dominant in the financing intra-European trade. Long-dated bills, issued by "agency houses" in the Anglo-Indian trade were typical for the Inter-continental trade.(Chapman, Stanley, 1984)

---

[3] *The Napoleonic Wars* (1803–1815) were a series of major global conflicts pitting the French Empire and its allies, led by Napoleon I, against a fluctuating array of European states formed into various coalitions.

At the beginning of 20th century the inland bill disappeared from circulation after the transformation of London discount market into international market. The instruments, used to finance domestic, intra-continental, and inter-continental trade unified. (Nishimura, Shizuya, 1971) Bills of exchange drawn by agents from all over the world became traded on the London discount market.

Specialized intermediaries known as "acceptance houses" established abroad, appeared in London. In order to allow their customers to borrow from investors in the London bill market, they guaranteed (accepted) bills on their account.

Investment in the bill market was stimulated by the Bank of England. By setting formal and informal rules, as a result of its lending-of-last-resort policy the British central bank encouraged the production of credit instruments on the market. By reducing the credit and liquidity risk associated with bills the bank supported their usage as an international "safe asset" on the London bill market.

The role of London as the world's trade center was kept unmatched in the period from 1870 to 1914. By the adoption of international gold standard the bill on London, drawn from any country, but payable by a London acceptor and eligible for rediscount at the Bank of England, transformed into the most widely demanded short-term financial instrument in the world. (Lindert, Peter, H., 1969) Diversity of investors - English financial institutions and investment trusts, foreign central and commercial banks, invested in sterling bills to finance global trade boom of 1870-1914. At the beginning of the 19th century the depth of the London discount market stimulated the appearance of "bill brokers" or discount houses. Buying bills of exchange they financed themselves through short-term deposits and credits from commercial banks. (King, Wilfred T.C., 1936) The locations of the importing and exporting firms and that of the lenders disconnected. British and foreign investors could lend funds to borrowers located in any country and finance a trade transaction from all over the world through the platform of the London market.

Any formal modification in the legal status of the bill of exchange could not be found in parallel with the remarkable transformation of the London discount market between its emergence as a domestic platform in the mid-18th century and as an international one in the late 19th century.

The Bills of Exchange Act of 1882 is the only important initiative in that period ratifying the already existing practices and rules codified by the common law courts during the 17th and early 18th centuries.(Geva, Benjamin, 2011)

The introduction of the principle of negotiability in 16th century Antwerp was the only significant legal change in the history of Western trade finance. Both acceptance houses and the Bank of England contributed to set eligibility standards for access to the market by outsiders as informal regulation in Britain and merchant banks and banks of issue established domestic standards on the Continent. (Ugolini, Stefano, 2017)

5.3 The Collapse of Global Trade Finance in the period of 1914-1939.

- *The First World War and the disruption in the London money market.*

During the First World War and interwar years the leading role of London in the global trade finance market progressively declined. London discount market was seriously influenced by the war.

> The political developments of the summer 1914 affected the City. The July crisis led some continental countries to declare moratoria on foreign exchange payments and to close their Stock Exchanges before Britain declared war on Germany.(Roberts, Richard, 2013)

As a result of the capital control foreign debtors who had drawn bills of exchange on leading acceptance houses or banks of London could not remit funds to these institutions to reimburse their credits. Some houses that had accepted/guaranteed large amounts of bills were unable to assume their liabilities.

Britain avoided a banking crisis after the strong measures of the British Government and Bank of England, but the liquidity of the world`s most widespread trade finance instrument – the sterling bill – had been destroyed. Restrictions on capital flows and war time difficulties in the management of international trade became the reasons for reducing the role of London as a global trade finance center.

- *Trade Finance Rebirth in the 1920s. The double-natured Market Structure.*

After the First World War the United States emerged as the largest creditor country and the world`s leading commercial power. The global trade finance market restored over the instruments from the 19th centuries. In the mid-1920s greater part of the European currencies stabilized. International trade, capital flows and the demand for credit from the importing and exporting firms substantially raised second half of the decade.

After removing the restrictions on US national banks' and Federal Reserve[4] member banks' acceptance activities by the Federal Reserve Act of 1913, a market for dollar denominated bankers' acceptances developed in New York. The dominance of London discount market was provoked by the appearance of another large acceptance market in New York. The US acceptance market was dominated by the country's largest commercial banks and directly supported from the monetary authorities in contrast to London where the largest share of bankers' acceptances was issued by small acceptance houses specialized in trade finance. (Accominotti, Olivier, 2012)

At the end of the 1920s, the volume of dollar bankers' acceptances rose substantially and the structure of the global trade finance market divided into two – London and New York fell in competition for the financing of international trade.

After the stabilization of the European currencies in 1920s, a great part of the related credit demand still remained run by the London City. In 1930 New York and London were financing equal parts of the global trade. The intensive competition between the banks in the two centers in the global acceptance market resulted in lowering fees charged in exchange for the guarantees and in a cutback in the standards set by intermediaries and monetary authorities.

- *The World Economic Crisis and the Collapse of Trade Finance in the 1930s.*

As a result of the World economic crisis of the 1930s the world trade collapsed, the world income declined in parallel with the reduction of the world export. Between 1929 and 1933, world export declined by almost 30 percent in real terms and this considerably reduced the demand for financing from firms. (Federico, Giovanni, and Antonio Tena-Junguito, 2016) The revival of acceptance finance of the 1920s was for a short time.

On the other hand the supply of trade finance was influenced by the financial crisis of the 1930s. In the summer of 1931 Germany and Central European countries imposed capital controls. Intermediating trade finance for continental customers the acceptance houses of the London City were heavily influenced by the international economic situation. (Accominotti, Olivier, 2012) Dominated by the largest commercial banks the acceptance business in the United States was less affected by the European crisis. Decreasing its holdings of bankers' acceptances to reinforce the dollar's

---

[4] *The Federal Reserve System* (also known as the Federal Reserve or simply the Fed) is the central banking system of the United States of America. It was created on December 23, 1913, with the enactment of the Federal Reserve Act, after a series of financial panics (particularly the panic of 1907) led to the desire for central control of the monetary system in order to alleviate financial crises.

gold parity the Federal Reserve withdrew the support to the New York acceptance market in 1931. The expansion of the market was hold. (Eichengreen, Barry, and Marc Flandreau, 2012)

In the second half of the 1930s the global trading system started to reorganize. Quantitative restrictions on trade flows and bilateral agreements[5] were established in many countries with Central European and Latin American countries. As a result state interference in international trade increased and cross-border credits declined. The share in the world export financed by New York and London discount market fell to 25 percent, in comparison with 43 percent in 1930.

Being the most important money market instrument in the interwar period the private firm's debt bankers' acceptances were replaced by the government debt Treasury bills. During The First World War the volume of Treasury bills, issued by the British authorities, rose significant.

In contrast with the weakening bill of exchange system the Convention on the Uniform Law of International Bills of Exchange, as one of attempts of establishing a uniform international financial regulation, was signed in Geneva in 1930. Being relatively similar to the English convention but with some formal differences, Anglo-Saxon countries refused to ratify the Convention. Its establishment as a uniform international legal standard was prevented.

> In 1988, the United Nations Commission on International Trade Law (UNCITRAL) tried to fill the loophole in the regulation of payment instruments by seeking convergence between the Anglo-American and Continental legal traditions. Although approved by the General Assembly on 9th December 1989, the resulting United Nations Convention on International Bills of Exchange and International Promissory Notes never entered into force, having been ratified by no country to date. (Moshenskyi, Sergii,2008) (Murray, Daniel,1994)

5.4 Trade Finance after the Second World War.

- *Trade Finance in the Bretton Woods Years in the period of 1944-1971.*

At the end of the Second World War international trade resumed and the old channels restarted to finance trade activities. The acceptance business of London trade and clearing banks and American commercial banks started

---

[5] These agreements were based on the principle of reciprocal trade and left the management of the bilateral trade balance to a government agency or compensation office.

again to provide trade credits to domestic and foreign exporters and importers.

The Bretton Woods conference in 1944 organized a system of fixed exchange rates to the US dollar as a dominant currency, and countries maintained restrictions on international capital movements. (Eichengreen, Barry, 1996) Many of the bilateral clearing agreements established in the 1930s continued to operate after the war.

Until the end of Bretton Woods international trade and finance remained regulated by state authorities. Over the 1950s and 1960s the restrictions to foreign lending were removed and current account convertibility was restored.

- *Trade Finance in the post-Bretton Woods Years in the period of 1973-1985.*

Capital controls were removed after the collapse of the Bretton Woods system in 1971-1973. The demand for trade finance rose after the revival in international trade in the late 1970s and early 1980s. In the post-Bretton Woods years the US dollar had consolidated its position as the dominant international currency since the United States was at the center of the global trading system through the US market, used by the exporters and importers to finance their trade activities.

In the late 1970s the US bankers' acceptance market experienced a new boom. The US banking regulation made the activity of accepting bills an attractive business for American banks. In 1973 the acceptances became free from reserve requirements. (Jensen, Frederik H., and Patrick M. Parkinson, 1986) Around 17% of world exports were financed though US bankers' acceptances in 1982-1984.

The New York market never resumed its importance in financing of world trade it had had at the end of the 1920s. The issuance of US dollar bankers' acceptances constantly declined after 1985. First, the growth of the commercial paper market allowed large corporations to borrow directly from non-financial investors and without the signature/guarantee of a US money-center bank. Second, acceptances lost their privileged regulatory status. Other forms of short-term asset-backed commercial paper got free from capital requirements at the end of 1990. (LaRoche, Robert K., 1993) The issuance of acceptances became less attractive activity for US financial institutions. From 1980s onwards the role of American banks became marginal.

- *Trade Finance after 1985.*

The trade finance infrastructure is completely different in the late 20th century in comparison with the global platform such as that developed in London over the course of the 19th century. The methods of financing have evolved. The international trade is financed by the intermediation of local banks in the exporting and importing firms' countries as it was at the origin of this market.

Initially exporters and importers rely on inter-firm trade credit. The exporters finance directly (the open account method) or the importers pre-pay (cash in advance/pre-payment method) the trade transaction. National and global banks provide direct loans and overdraft facilities to firms in need of working capital. (Cooper, Stuart, and Inke Nyborg, 1997) Large corporations also borrow in the US or Euro commercial paper markets. (Asmundson, Irena, Thomas William Dorsey, Armine Khachatryan, Ioana Niculcea, and Mika Saito, 2011)

To insure exporters against importers' default risk, banks offer specific trade finance products such as letter of credit and documentary collections. (Amiti, Mary, and David E. Weinstein, 2011) The bank of the importer issues a letter of credit guaranteeing the exporter that payment should be made against presentation of a set of documents proving the shipment of goods. The confirmation by the exporter bank adds another guarantee to the payment in the letter of credit product. The exporter often postpones the payment from the importer by selling the acceptance of the letter of credit by the issuing bank at a discount.

By contrast, in the case of documentary collection banks are only transferring the documents from the exporter to the importer and assisting in the collection of payment. (Asmundson, Irena, Thomas William Dorsey, Armine Khachatryan, Ioana Niculcea, and Mika Saito, 2011), The exporters provide the insurance from non-bank, insurance companies against importers' payment default or receive guarantees from export credit agencies. (Bank for International Settlements, 2014)

The structure of the late 20th century global trade finance is different from that of the 19th century. In the nineteenth century the world trade finance passed through the London financial center. While nowadays national banks or branches of global banks situated in the exporter's and importer's country are the intermediaries in trade finance services. Centralization around London before the First World War determined the implicit regulation of trade finance services by the Bank of England. The regulation of local and global banks nowadays is in priority of national authorities. The decentralized organization of international trade finance nowadays resembles the organization at the origins of the market in the medieval period, reminding of the international pre-eminence of Italian and

South-German banking groups in the late middle Ages. (De Roover, Raymond, 1953)

When the banking system is not so developed, a phenomenon known as the "trade finance gap", it is possible local firms to suffer from a lack of intermediation. (Asmundson, Irena, Thomas William Dorsey, Armine Khachatryan, Ioana Niculcea, and Mika Saito, 2011) The trade finance of such firms might be more vulnerable to shocks to the domestic financial system. During the crisis of the 1990s the reduction of the export of the Japanese firms was stronger than the others. (Amiti, Mary, and David E. Weinstein, 2011) Many researchers (Ahn, JaeBin, Mary Amiti, and David E. Weinstein, 2011) (Del Prete, Silvia, and Stefano Federico, 2014) (Paravisini, Daniel, Veronica Rappoport, Philipp Schnabl, and Daniel Wolfenzon, 2015) have investigated the effects of global financial crisis of 2008-2009 over the supply of trade finance. The credit restrictions affected firms engaging in international trade and a collapse in the world trade followed in the year after the crisis.

The other characteristic of the today's trade finance market is the level of credit securitization. The establishment of bills of exchange negotiability accelerated their usage as a trade transaction financing instrument around the world in the sixteenth century. In the nineteenth century and interwar period and to a lesser extent in the 1970s and 1980s, bankers' acceptances drawn by firms around the world on leading financial houses in London and New York were used as money market instruments and traded by different types of bank and non-bank investors. From 1980s the trends has changed and the usage of trade finance products for money market transactions reduced. Due to the lack of standardization and knowledge of this type of products, the demand for them from non-bank investors stays restricted, while global banks made attempts to securitize their trade finance portfolios or specific trade finance credits. There are two ultimate sources for international trade transactions finance nowadays – one relying on inter-firm credit or not discounted by the exporter's bank letter of credit and the other from the bank of the exporter or the importer (in case of a letter of credit with a working capital loan). (Bank for International Settlements, 2014) Providers of capital for the financing of international trade today are represented mainly by local banks being in direct contact with borrowing firms. In comparison with pre-First World War period, when investors in bills of exchange were of different types without having any specific knowledge of the last borrower.

5.5 The evolution of short-term and medium-term trade finance in the 2020s.

The trade finance industry is highly influenced by factors affecting international trade and the money supply. Less trade means less potential business to finance. At the same time the rising trade risk can be the reason for increasing demand for risk mitigation instruments, such as credit insurance or guarantees. The aggregate demand and the financing conditions of trading firms can be affected similarly by the changes in monetary and fiscal policies.

- *Surging the credit of the private sector.*

Central banks around the world struggle with the negative impact of the pandemic on the global economy using different policy tools to maintain borrowing, to support access to credit to business and households. The targeted groups started from different level of governments (from central to local), various sizes of businesses (small and medium enterprises to large corporations) to households and non-profit organizations. The instruments included: keeping the interest rates at historical low levels and forward guidance to stabilize expectations; quantitative easing by purchasing treasury and mortgage-back securities; lending to financial firms, purchases of corporate securities, direct lending to nonfinancial firms, international swap lines among others to keep the liquidity provision and credit support; reductions of reserve requirements for lending, lower standards for collateral.

*Households` savings highly increased as a result of fiscal transfers, short-term working schemes and tax measures used in several economies.* The financial support to businesses` cash-flow and households` income and employment provided by governments included: loans, debt guarantees or equity injections to support businesses activities and employment; job retention schemes; deferral of tax, rent, utilities payments and social security contributions, and debt moratorium; paid sick leave; direct lump sum payment and increase of unemployment benefit payments. As a result, credit to non-financial institutions raised by 8% of GDP in Eurozone countries, 6% in the United States, and 15% of GDP in emerging economies and credit to households increased by 3 and 8% of GDP for advanced and emerging economies. (OECD,2021)

- *Short-term trade finance declined in 2020 against medium-trade finance expansion.*

The demand of short-term trade finance declined in 2020 after the contraction of the demand and supply of merchandises trade as a result of the Covid-19 crises. Short-term trade finance exposure declined by 21% to the amount of USD 2,043 billion after the large reduction of merchandises imports and exports. (ICC, 2021) Trade loans and import letters of credit contracted by 23% and 29%, respectively.

Banks from the private sector restricted the supply of short-term finance. According to the data from the 2021 ICC Trade Register the lower supply of liquidity from the banking sector determined the decline (75% of total exposure) in short-term trade finance products in 2020, a decrease in the number of borrowers for trade loans (-8%) and letters of credit (-18% for imports, -9% for exports) and a reduction of the median amount for trade loans by 30% from USD169 to 129 million. In the beginning of 2020 a liquidity withdrawal was also caused by the rising Treasury-Eurodollar rate (TED) spread from 0.4 in the beginning of the lockdown to the peak of 1.4 at the end of March 2020. The restrictive trend of the lending market to the private sector might also be strengthened by the Basel and solvency requirements.

In combination with credit insurance or guarantees as additional government's support medium-term trade finance (or export finance) has been comparatively more flexible in comparison with short-term trade finance. The raising of medium-term trade finance has been 26% reaching USD 65billion between 2019 and 2020 - 70% of the increase covered by the corporate loans, followed by the sovereign loans.(ICC, 2021) To support trade and to fill the trade financing gap through the Export Credit Agencies governments implemented different measures as: boosting their working capital support programs; introducing export credit insurance or guarantees; improving the flexibility for repayments, interest rates, fees, claims; improving the policy approval, contactless application processes, provided deadline extensions and extended time for notification and filing claims.

Trade finance kept its low-risk profile in the turbulence times. The trade collapse provoked by the lockdowns doubled the value of defaults for short-term trade finance to reach USD 5.5billion between 2019 and 2020. The trend was determined by trade loans defaults amounted 80% of the increase. The default rate as a percentage of total exposure stayed low and reached 0.3% in 2020 while global non-performing loans exceeded 6% in 2020 and during the global financial crisis in 2009/2010.

Summery

From long-term perspective on international trade finance similar instruments stayed in use more than eight centuries. The bill of exchange has proven to be extremely flexible. Its transformation over time reflected the evolution of global trade finance market. Starting from localized bank-intermediated medieval bills of exchange, the appearance of the negotiable bill of exchange allowed trade finance instruments to circulate more widely during the early modern times. The standardization of bills (or acceptances) turned the London acceptance market into the world's important money market. In the interwar period and the period after the Second World War the acceptance market declined and could not recover after the new boom in the international trade after 1980. Nowadays the structure of trade finance market is the same as it was the case at its origin. Local banks and local branches of global banks offer a range of products to firms.

In the nineteenth century the main trade suppliers were located in London and subject to the authority of the Bank of England. The governance and regulation of trade finance by Britain as the leading political power was challenged during the interwar period when London acceptance houses fell into competition with the big US trade banks.

Nowadays, firm's access to trade finance credits are defined on a local basis, while regulation of banks offering trade finance products is left to national authorities. In combination with credit insurance or guarantees as additional government's support medium-term trade finance (or export finance) has been comparatively more flexible in comparison with short-term trade finance. Trade finance kept its low-risk profile in the turbulence times.

Literature:

Accominotti, Olivier (2012), "London Merchant Banks, the Central European Panic and the Sterling Crisis of 1931", The Journal of Economic History, vol.72, pp.1-43.

Adelino, M., M.Ferriera, M. Giannetti and P.Pires (2020): *"Trade Credit and the Transmission of Unconventional Monetary Policy"*, NBER Working Papers, no.27077.

Ahn, J.B., and Sarmiento, M. (2019), *"Estimating the Direct Impact of Bank Liquidity Shocks on the Real Economy: Evidence from Letter of Credit Import Transactions in Columbia"*, Review of International Economics, Review Papers & Proceedings, 27, 1510-36.

Ahn, JaeBin (2011), *"A Theory of Domestic and International Trade Finance"*, IMF Working Papers, No 11/262.

Ahn, JaeBin, Mary Amiti, and David E. Weinstein (2011), "Trade Finance and the Great Trade Collapse", American Economic Review Papers and Proceedings, vol. 101, pp. 298-302.

Amiti, Mary and David E. Weinstein (2011), *"Exports and Financial Shocks"*, The Quarterly Journal of Economics (2011), Vol. 126 (4), pp. 1841-1877.

Amiti, Mary, and David E. Weinstein (2011), "Exports and Financial Shocks", Quarterly Journal of Economics, vol. 126, pp. 1841-1877.

Amiti, Mary, and David E. Weinstein (2011), "Exports and Financial Shocks", Quarterly Journal of Economics, vol. 126, pp. 1841-1877.

Antras, Pol and Fritz Foley (2011), *"Poultry in Motion: A Study of International Trade Finance Practices"*, NBER Working Paper no.17091.

Asian Development Bank (ADB, 2019), *"2019 Trade Finance Gaps, Growth, and Jobs Survey"*, No.113, September, 2019.

Asmundson, Irena, Thomas William Dorsey, Armine Khachatryan, Ioana Niculcea, and Mika Saito

Auboin, M. and M.Meier-Ewert (2008), *Improving the availability of trade finance during financial crises,* World Trade Organisation, https://www.wto.org/english/res_e/booksp_e/dis02_e.pdf

Avdjiev, S., W.DU, C. Koch and H.S.Shin (2019), "*The Dollar, Bank Levarage, and Deviations from Covered Interest parity*", American Economic Review Insights, vol.1, pp, 193-208.

Bank for International Settlements (2014), "Trade Finance: Developments and Issues", CGFS Papers No 50, January 2014.

Behrens, Kristian, Gregory Corcos, and Giordano Mion (2011) "*Trade Crisis? What Trade Crisis?*", CEPR Discussion Paper no. 7956.

Berman, N., Rebeyrol, V. and Vicard, V. (2019), "*Demand Learning and Firm Dynamics. Evidence from Exporters*", Review of Economics and Statistics, 101(1), 91-106.

Berman, Nicolas and Jerome Hericourt (2010), "*Financial Factors and the Margins of Trade: Evidence from Cross-country firm-level data*", Journal of Development Economics, Vol. 93, pp.206-217.

Boissay, F. and R.Gropp (2013), "*Payment Defaults and Interim Liquidity Provision*", Review of Finance, vol.17, pp.1653-94.

Boissay, F., N. Patel and H.Song Shin (2020), "*Trade Credit, Trade Finance, and the Covid-19 Crisis*", BIS Bulletin, no.24, 19 June.

Bricongne, Jean-Charles, Lionel Fontagne, Guillaume Gaulier, Daria Taglioni, and Vincent Vicard (2012), "*Firms and the Global Crisis: French Exports in the Turmoil*", Journal of International Economics, Vol.87, pp. 134-146.

Bruno, V. and H.S.Shin (2019), "*Dollar and Export*", BIS Working Papers, no.819.

Bruno, V., S-J Kim and H.S.Shin (2018): "*What`s Special about the Dollar in Financial Markets? Exchange Rates and the Working Capital Channels of Trade Fluctuations*", American Economic Association Papers and Proceedings, vol.108, pp.531-36.

Carstens, A. (2020), "*Bold Steps to Pump Coronavirus Rescue Funds down the Last Mile*", Financial Times, 29 March.

Chaney, Thomas (2005), "*Liquidity Constrained Exporters*", University of Chicago, mimeo.

Chapman, Stanley D. (1984), The Rise of Marchant Banking, London: Allen&Unwin.

Chauffour, J. and T.Faraole (2009), *Trade finance in crises: Market Adjustments or market failure?*, World Bank, https://documents.worldbank.org/curated/en/673931468336294560/Trade-finance-in-crisis-market-adjustments-or-market-failure.

Chor, Davin and Kalina Manova (2012), "*Off the Cliff and Back? Credit Conditions and International Trade during the Global Financial Crisis*", Journal of International Economics, Vol.87, pp.117-133.

Committee on the Global Financial System (2014), "*Trade Finance Developments and issues*", CGFS Papers, no.50.

Cooper, Stuart, and Inke Nyborg (1997), "The Financing and Information Needs of Smaller Exporters", Bank of England Quarterly Bulletin, Q2, pp. 166-172.

Coulibaly, B., H.Sapriza and A. Zlate (2011), "*Trade Credit and International Trade during the 2008-2009 Global Financial Crisis*", Board of Governors of the Federal Reserve System, *International Finance Discussion Papers,* no.50.

De Roover, Raymond (1953), L'evolution de la letter de change, XIVe-XVIIIe siecles, Paris: Armand Colin.

De Roover, Raymond (1953), L'evolution de la letter de change, XIVe-XVIIIe siecles, Paris: Armand Colin.

De Roover, Raymond (1974), "Cambium ad Venetias: Contribution to the History of Foreign Exchange", in Julius Kirsher (ed.), Business, Banking, and Economic Thought in Late Medieval and Early Modern Europe: Selected Studies of Raymond De Roover, Chicago and London: University of Chicago Press, pp. 239-259.

De Roover, Raymond, Money, Banking and Credit in Mediaeval Bruges (Cambridge, Mass. 1948), pp. 56, 72; from the Datini Archives of Prato, pp. 1146.

Del Prete, Silvia, and Stefano Federico (2014), "Trade and Finance: Is There More than Just "Trade Finance"? Evidence from Matched Bank-Firm Data", Bank of Italy Working Papers No 948, January 2014.

Demir, B., Michalski, T.K. and Ors, E. (2017), "*Risk-based Capital Requirements for Banks and International Trade*", The Review of Financial Studies, 30(11), 3970-4002.

Demir, Banu and Beata Javorcik (2018): "*Don't Throw in the Towel, Throw in Trade Credit*", Journal of International Economics, 111, 177-89.

Demir, Banu and Beata Javorcik (2020): "*Trade Finance Matters: Evidence from the COVID-19 Crisis*", Oxford Review of Economic Policy, Vol.36, November, 2020, pp.5397-8408.

Eaglesham, J. (2020), "*Supply Chaim Finance is a New Risk in Crisis*", Wall Street Journal, 4 April

Eaton, J., Kortum, S., Neiman, B., and Romalis, J.(2016), "*Trade and the Global Recession*", American Economic Review, 106(11), 3401-38.

Eck, Katharina, Martina Engemann, and Monika Schnitzer (2012), "*How Trade Credits Foster International Trade*", CEPR Discussion Paper no.8954.

Egger, Peter and Thomas Url (2006), "*Public Export Credit Guarantees and Foreign Trade Structure: Evidence from Austria*", The World Economy, Vol. 29, No.4, pp.399-418.

Eichengreen, Barry (1996), Globalizing Capital: A History of the International Monetary System, Princeton NJ: Princeton University Press.

Eichengreen, Barry, and Marc Flandreau (2012), "The Federal Reserve, the Bank of England, and the Rise of the Dollar as an International Currency, 1914-1939", Open Economies Review, vol.23, pp.57-87.

Ellingsen, T., & Vlachos, J. (2009). *Trade Finance During Liquidity Crisis*. International Trade Department, The World Bank. Mimeo.

Evenett, S. (2009), "Crisis-era Protectionism One Year after the Washington G30 Meeting", ch.5 in R.Baldwin (ed.), The Great Trade Collapse: Causes, Consequences and Prospect, VoxEUorg, 37-45.

Fabbri, D., & Klapper, L.(2009). *Trade credit and the Supply Chain (February 2009)*, Development Research Group, The World Bank.

Fabbri, D., & Menichini, A. (2009). *Trade Credit, Collateral Liquidation, and Borrowing Constraints (January 2009)*.

Federico, Giovanni, and Antonio Tena-Junguito (2016), "World Trade, 1800-1938: A New Data-Set", EHES Working Paper No93 (January 2016).

Felbermayr, Gabriel and Erdal Yalcin (2011), "*Export Credit Guarantees and Export Performance: An Empirical Analysis for Germany*", Ifo Working Paper No.116.

Financial Times, http://www.ft.com/content/c8a13e05-f47f-410a-898b-af3d758d7a6e, 28 April 2020.

Fisman, Raymond and Inessa Love (2003), "*Trade Credit, Financial Intermediary Development, and Industry Growth*", The Journal of Finance, Vol. 58, No. 1 (Feb.,2003), pp. 353-374.

Flandreau, Marc, and Clemens Jobst (2005), "The Ties That Divide: A Network Analysis of the International Monetary System, 1890-1910", The Journal of Economic History, vol.65, pp.977-1007.

Geva, Benjamin (2011), *The Payment Order of Antiquity and the Middle Ages: A Legal History*, Oxford and Portland OR: Hart Publishing.

Giannitti, M., Burkart, M., & Ellingsen, T. (2007). *What you Sell is What you Lend? Explaining Trade Credit Contracts (September 2007)*. EFA 2006 Zurich Meetings; ECGI – Finance Research Paper No. 71/2005.

Gillard, Lucien (2004), La Banque d'Amsterdam et le florin europeen au temps de la Republique neerlandaise (1610-1820), Paris:EHESS.

Glady, Nicolas and Jacques Potin (2011), *"Bank Intermediation and Default Risk in International Trade – Theory and Evidence"*, ESSEC Business School, mimeo.

https://doi.org/10.1787/97a5bbfe-en

https://icc-trade-financing-covid19.pdf

https://voxeu.org/article/economic-policy-under-pandemic-european-perspective

https://www.oecd.org/economic-outlook/march-2021/

Iacovone, Leonardo and Veronica Zavacka (2009), *"Banking Crisis and Exports: Lessons from the Past"*, Policy Research Working Paper Series 5016, The World Bank.

International Chamber of Commerce (2018), *"Global Risk in Trade Finance"*, Trade Register Report.

International Chamber of Commerce (2018), *"ICC Global Survey 2018: Securing future growth"*, Global Survey Report, https://iccwbo.org/publication/global-survey-2018-securing-future-growth/

International Chamber of Commerce (2020), *"Trade Financing and Covid-19"*, May 2020.

International Chamber of Commerce, "2021 Trade register report, Global risks in Trade Finance", 2021.

Jafari, P. and J.Kalousova, (2018),"*Payables Finance: What Can We Learn from the Abengoa and Carillon Experiances?"*, International; Trade and Forfaiting Association, report.

Jensen, Frederik H., and Patrick M. Parkinson (1986) "Recent Developments in the Bankers' Acceptance Market", Federal Reserve Bulletin, vol. 72 (January 1986), pp. 1-12.

John Hassier, P. (Jul 2020), *Economic Policy under the Pandemic: A European Perspective,*

Kim, S-J and H.S.Shin (2012):"*Sustaining Production Chains through Financial Linkages*", American Economic Review Papers and Proceedings, vol.102, no 3, pp. 402-6.

King, Wilfred T.C. (1936), History of the London Discount Market, London: Routledge.

Kiyoaki, N.,& Moore. J. (1997). *Credit Cycles.* Journal of Political Economy, 105, 211-248.

LaRoche, Robert K. (1993) "Bankers Acceptances", Federal Reserve Bank of Richmond Economic Quarterly, vol. 79 (Winter 1993), pp. 75-85.

Levchenko, Andrei A., Logan T. Lewis, and Linda L., Tesar (2010), "*The Collapse of International Trade During the 2008-2009 Crisis: In Search of the Smoking Gun*", NBER Working Paper no.16006.

Lindert, Peter, H. (1969), "Key Currencies and Gold, 1900-1913", Princeton Studies in International Finance, No 24, pp.1-85.

Lotte van Wersch, C.(2019), *Statistical coverage of trade finance – Fintechs and supply chain financing*, http://file.///C:/Users/schleich_j/Downloads/wpiea2019165-print-pdf.pdf.

Love, Inessa, Lorenzo A. Preve, and Virginia Sarria-Allende (2007), "*Trade Credit and Bank Credit: Evidence from Recent Financial Crisis* ", Journal of Financial Economics, Vol.83, pp.453-469.

Manova, Kalina (2013), *"Credit Constraints, Heterogeneous Firms, and International Trade"*, Stanford University, mimeo.

Melitz, Marc (2003), *"The Impact of Trade on Intra-Industry Reallocations and Aggregate Industry Productivity"*, Econometrica 71, pp.1695-1725.

Meltzer, Allan H. (1960), "*Mercantile Credit, Monetary Policy, and Size of Firms*", The Review of Economics and Statistics, Vol.42, No.4(Nov., 1960), pp. 429-437.

Menichini, A. (2009), *Study of Inter-firm Trade Finance in Times of Crisis.* International Trade Department, The World Bank. Mimeo.

Miller, J., D.Keohane, C. Bushey and P.Campbell (2020): "*Weakest Link in Supply Chaim Threatens Car Industry Revival*", Financial Times, 16 April.

Moser, Christph, Thorsten Nestmann, and Michael Wedow (2008), "*Political Risk and Export Promotion: Evidence from Germany*", The World Economy, Vol. 31, No. 6, pp.781-803.

Moshenskyi, Sergii (2008), History of the Weksel: Bill of Exchange and Promissory Note, Bloomington IN:Xlibris., pp.172-174.

Mueller, Reinhold C. (1997), The Venetian Money Market: Banks, Panics and the Public Debt, 1200-1500, Baltimore MD: Johns Hopkins University Press.

Murray, Daniel E. (1994), "The U.N. Convention on International Bills of Exchange and International

Niepmann, E., and Schmidt-Eisenlohr, T., (2017), *"International Trade, Risk and the Role of Banks"*, Journal of international Economics, 107, 111-26.

Nilsen, Jeffrey H. (2002), *"Trade Credit and the ank Lending Channel"*, Journal of Money, Credit and Banking, Vol. 34, No.1 (Feb.,2002), pp.226-253.

Nishimura, Shizuya (1971), The Decline of Inland Bills of Exchange in the London Money Market, 1855-1913, Cambridge: Cambridge University Press.

OECD (2020), *OECD Economic Outlook, Volume 2020 Issue 2*, OECD Publishing, Paris, https://doi.org/10.1787/16097408

OECD (2020): *"Trade Finance in Times of Crisis – Responses from Export Credit Agencies"*, OECD Policy responses to Coronavirus.

OECD (Mar 2021*)*, *"Economic Outlook, Interim Report"*

OECD, "OECD SME and Entrepreneurship Outlook 2021", OECD Publishing, Paris,2021,

Otsen, Morten (2010), *"Banks in International Trade& Incomplete International Contract Enforcement and Reputational Concerns ,"* Harvard University, mimeo.

Paravisini, Daniel, Veronica Rappoport, Philipp Schnabl, and Daniel Wolfenzon (2015), "Dissecting the Effect of Credit Supply on Trade: Evidence from Matched Credit-Export Data", Review of Economic Studies, vol. 82, pp. 333-359.

Paravisini, Daniel, Veronica Rapport, Philipp Schnabl, and Daniel Wolfenzon (2011), *"Dissecting the effect of Credit Supply on Trade: Evidence from Matched Credit-Export Data"*, NBER Working Paper no.16975.

Petersen, M & Raghuram, G. (1997), *Trade Credit: Theory and Evidence*. Review of Financial Studies, 10(3), 661-691.

Promissory Notes with Some Comparisons with the Former and Revised Article Three of the UCC", University of Miami Inter-American Law Review, vol. 25, pp. 189-225.

Raddatz, C. (2008). *Credit Chains and Sectoral Comovement: Does the Use of Trade Credit Amplify Sectoral Shocks?* (February 2008). Development Research Group, The World Bank.

Roberts, Richard (2013), Saving the City: The Great Financial Crisis of 1914, Oxford: Oxford University Press.

Shmidt-Eisenlohr, Tim (2013), *"Towards a Theory of Trade Finance"*, Journal of International Economics, 91(1). 96-112.

Ugolini, Stefano (2017), The Evolution of Central Banking: Theory and History, London: Palgrave Macmillan.

Van der Veer, Koen (2010), *"The Private Credit Insurance Effect on Trade"*, DNB Working Paper No.264.

World Trade Organization (2020), *"Trade set to plunge as COVID-19 pandemic upends global economy"*, 8 April, 2020.

WTO and IFC (2019), *"Trade Finance and the Compliance Challenges"*, A Showcase of International Corporation, Geneva and Washington, DC, World Trade Organization and International Finance Corporation.

www.ingramcontent.com/pod-product-compliance
Lightning Source LLC
Chambersburg PA
CBHW031554210526
45464CB00003B/1297